4405
3

Wie ist das klein, womit wir ringen;
was mit uns ringt, wie ist das gross . . .

LOUISE BOGAN

The Blue Estuaries

POEMS: 1923–1968

FARRAR, STRAUS & GIROUX

NEW YORK

To the memory of my father, mother and brother

CONTENTS

II

III

IV

V

VI

I

A TALE

This youth too long has heard the break
Of waters in a land of change.
He goes to see what suns can make
From soil more indurate and strange.

He cuts what holds his days together
And shuts him in, as lock on lock:
The arrowed vane announcing weather,
The tripping racket of a clock;

Seeking, I think, a light that waits
Still as a lamp upon a shelf,—
A land with hills like rocky gates
Where no sea leaps upon itself.

But he will find that nothing dares
To be enduring, save where, south
Of hidden deserts, torn fire glares
On beauty with a rusted mouth,—

Where something dreadful and another
Look quietly upon each other.

MEDUSA

I had come to the house, in a cave of trees,
Facing a sheer sky.
Everything moved,—a bell hung ready to strike,
Sun and reflection wheeled by.

When the bare eyes were before me
And the hissing hair,
Held up at a window, seen through a door.
The stiff bald eyes, the serpents on the forehead
Formed in the air.

This is a dead scene forever now.
Nothing will ever stir.
The end will never brighten it more than this,
Nor the rain blur.

The water will always fall, and will not fall,
And the tipped bell make no sound.
The grass will always be growing for hay
Deep on the ground.

And I shall stand here like a shadow
Under the great balanced day,
My eyes on the yellow dust, that was lifting in the wind,
And does not drift away.

SUB CONTRA

Notes on the tuned frame of strings
Plucked or silenced under the hand
Whimper lightly to the ear,
Delicate and involute,
Like the mockery in a shell.
Lest the brain forget the thunder
The roused heart once made it hear,—
Rising as that clamor fell,—
Let there sound from music's root
One note rage can understand,
A fine noise of riven things.
Build there some thick chord of wonder;
Then, for every passion's sake,
Beat upon it till it break.

THE FRIGHTENED MAN

In fear of the rich mouth
I kissed the thin,—
Even that was a trap
To snare me in.

Even she, so long
The frail, the scentless,
Is become strong
And proves relentless.

O, forget her praise,
And how I sought her
Through a hazardous maze
By shafted water.

BETROTHED

You have put your two hands upon me, and your mouth,
You have said my name as a prayer.
Here where trees are planted by the water
I have watched your eyes, cleansed from regret,
And your lips, closed over all that love cannot say.

My mother remembers the agony of her womb
And long years that seemed to promise more than this.
She says, "You do not love me,
You do not want me,
You will go away."

In the country whereto I go
I shall not see the face of my friend
Nor her hair the color of sunburnt grasses;
Together we shall not find
The land on whose hills bends the new moon
In air traversed of birds.

What have I thought of love?
I have said, "It is beauty and sorrow."
I have thought that it would bring me lost delights, and splendor
As a wind out of old time. . . .

But there is only the evening here,
And the sound of willows
Now and again dipping their long oval leaves in the water.

AD CASTITATEM

I make the old sign.
I invoke you,
Chastity
Life moves no more
A breeze of flame.
Alike upon the ground
Struck by the same withering
Lie the fruitful and the barren branch.
Alike over them
Closes the mould.
I call upon you,
Who have not known you;
I invoke you,
Stranger though I be.
Against this blackened heart
I hold your offerings—
Water, and a stone.

In this ravaged country,
In this season not yours,
You having no season,
I call upon you without echo.
Hear me, infertile,
Beautiful futility.

KNOWLEDGE

Now that I know
How passion warms little
Of flesh in the mould,
And treasure is brittle,—

I'll lie here and learn
How, over their ground,
Trees make a long shadow
And a light sound.

JUAN'S SONG

When beauty breaks and falls asunder
I feel no grief for it, but wonder.
When love, like a frail shell, lies broken,
I keep no chip of it for token.
I never had a man for friend
Who did not know that love must end.
I never had a girl for lover
Who could discern when love was over.
What the wise doubt, the fool believes—
Who is it, then, that love deceives?

PORTRAIT

She has no need to fear the fall
Of harvest from the laddered reach
Of orchards, nor the tide gone ebbing
      From the steep beach.

Nor hold to pain's effrontery
Her body's bulwark, stern and savage,
Nor be a glass, where to foresee
      Another's ravage.

What she has gathered, and what lost,
She will not find to lose again.
She is possessed by time, who once
      Was loved by men.

THE ROMANTIC

Admit the ruse to fix and name her chaste
With those who sleep the spring through, one and one,
Cool nights, when laurel builds up, without haste,
Its precise flower, like a pentagon.

In her obedient breast, all that ran free
You thought to bind, like echoes in a shell.
At the year's end, you promised, it would be
The unstrung leaves, and not her heart, that fell.

So the year broke and vanished on the screen
You cast about her; summer went to haws.
This, by your leave, is what she should have been,—
Another man will tell you what she was.

MY VOICE NOT BEING PROUD

My voice, not being proud
Like a strong woman's, that cries
Imperiously aloud
That death disarm her, lull her—
Screams for no mourning color
Laid menacingly, like fire,
Over my long desire.
It will end, and leave no print.
As you lie, I shall lie:
Separate, eased and cured.
Whatever is wasted or wanted
In this country of glass and flint
Some garden will use, once planted.
As you lie alone, I shall lie,
O, in singleness assured,
Deafened by mire and lime.
I remember, while there is time.

STATUE AND BIRDS

Here, in the withered arbor, like the arrested wind,
Straight sides, carven knees,
Stands the statue, with hands flung out in alarm
Or remonstrances.

Over the lintel sway the woven bracts of the vine
In a pattern of angles.
The quill of the fountain falters, woods rake on the sky
Their brusque tangles.

The birds walk by slowly, circling the marble girl,
The golden quails,
The pheasants, closed up in their arrowy wings,
Dragging their sharp tails.

The inquietudes of the sap and of the blood are spent.
What is forsaken will rest.
But her heel is lifted,—she would flee,—the whistle of the birds
Fails on her breast.

THE ALCHEMIST

I burned my life, that I might find
A passion wholly of the mind,
Thought divorced from eye and bone,
Ecstasy come to breath alone.
I broke my life, to seek relief
From the flawed light of love and grief.

With mounting beat the utter fire
Charred existence and desire.
It died low, ceased its sudden thresh.
I had found unmysterious flesh—
Not the mind's avid substance—still
Passionate beyond the will.

MEN LOVED WHOLLY BEYOND WISDOM

Men loved wholly beyond wisdom
Have the staff without the banner.
Like a fire in a dry thicket
Rising within women's eyes
Is the love men must return.
Heart, so subtle now, and trembling,
What a marvel to be wise,
To love never in this manner!
To be quiet in the fern
Like a thing gone dead and still,
Listening to the prisoned cricket
Shake its terrible, dissembling
Music in the granite hill.

THE CROWS

The woman who has grown old
And knows desire must die,
Yet turns to love again,
Hears the crows' cry.

She is a stem long hardened,
A weed that no scythe mows.
The heart's laughter will be to her
The crying of the crows,

Who slide in the air with the same voice
Over what yields not, and what yields,
Alike in spring, and when there is only bitter
Winter-burning in the fields.

MEMORY

Do not guard this as rich stuff without mark
Closed in a cedarn dark,
Nor lay it down with tragic masks and greaves,
Licked by the tongues of leaves.

Nor let it be as eggs under the wings
Of helpless, startled things,
Nor encompassed by song, nor any glory
Perverse and transitory.

Rather, like shards and straw upon coarse ground,
Of little worth when found,—
Rubble in gardens, it and stones alike,
That any spade may strike.

WOMEN

Women have no wilderness in them,
They are provident instead,
Content in the tight hot cell of their hearts
To eat dusty bread.

They do not see cattle cropping red winter grass,
They do not hear
Snow water going down under culverts
Shallow and clear.

They wait, when they should turn to journeys,
They stiffen, when they should bend.
They use against themselves that benevolence
To which no man is friend.

They cannot think of so many crops to a field
Or of clean wood cleft by an axe.
Their love is an eager meaninglessness
Too tense, or too lax.

They hear in every whisper that speaks to them
A shout and a cry.
As like as not, when they take life over their door-sills
They should let it go by.

LAST HILL IN A VISTA

Come, let us tell the weeds in ditches
How we are poor, who once had riches,
And lie out in the sparse and sodden
Pastures that the cows have trodden,
The while an autumn night seals down
The comforts of the wooden town.

Come, let us counsel some cold stranger
How we sought safety, but loved danger.
So, with stiff walls about us, we
Chose this more fragile boundary:
Hills, where light poplars, the firm oak,
Loosen into a little smoke.

STANZA

No longer burn the hands that seized
Small wreaths from branches scarcely green.
Wearily sleeps the hardy, lean
Hunger that could not be appeased.
The eyes that opened to white day
Watch cloud that men may look upon:
Leda forgets the wings of the swan;
Danaë has swept the gold away.

THE CHANGED WOMAN

The light flower leaves its little core
Begun upon the waiting bough.
Again she bears what she once bore
And what she knew she re-learns now.

The cracked glass fuses at a touch,
The wound heals over, and is set
In the whole flesh, and is not much
Quite to remember or forget.

Rocket and tree, and dome and bubble
Again behind her freshened eyes
Are treacherous. She need not trouble.
Her lids will know them when she dies.

And while she lives, the unwise, heady
Dream, ever denied and driven,
Will one day find her bosom ready,—
That never thought to be forgiven.

CHANSON UN PEU NAÏVE

What body can be ploughed,
Sown, and broken yearly?
She would not die, she vowed,
But she has, nearly.
   Sing, heart, sing;
   Call and carol clearly.

And, since she could not die,
Care would be a feather,
A film over the eye
Of two that lie together.
   Fly, song, fly,
   Break your little tether.

So from strength concealed
She makes her pretty boast:
Pain is a furrow healed
And she may love you most.
   Cry, song, cry,
   And hear your crying lost.

FIFTEENTH FAREWELL

I

You may have all things from me, save my breath,
The slight life in my throat will not give pause
For your love, nor your loss, nor any cause.
Shall I be made a panderer to death,
Dig the green ground for darkness underneath,
Let the dust serve me, covering all that was
With all that will be? Better, from time's claws,
The hardened face under the subtle wreath.

Cooler than stones in wells, sweeter, more kind
Than hot, perfidious words, my breathing moves
Close to my plunging blood. Be strong, and hang
Unriven mist over my breast and mind,
My breath! We shall forget the heart that loves,
Though in my body beat its blade, and its fang.

II

I erred, when I thought loneliness the wide
Scent of mown grass over forsaken fields,
Or any shadow isolation yields.
Loneliness was the heart within your side.
Your thought, beyond my touch, was tilted air
Ringed with as many borders as the wind.
How could I judge you gentle or unkind
When all bright flying space was in your care?

Now that I leave you, I shall be made lonely
By simple empty days,—never that chill
Resonant heart to strike between my arms
Again, as though distraught for distance,—only
Levels of evening, now, behind a hill,
Or a late cock-crow from the darkening farms.

SONNET

Since you would claim the sources of my thought
Recall the meshes whence it sprang unlimed,
The reedy traps which other hands have timed
To close upon it. Conjure up the hot
Blaze that it cleared so cleanly, or the snow
Devised to strike it down. It will be free.
Whatever nets draw in to prison me
At length your eyes must turn to watch it go.

My mouth, perhaps, may learn one thing too well,
My body hear no echo save its own,
Yet will the desperate mind, maddened and proud,
Seek out the storm, escape the bitter spell
That we obey, strain to the wind, be thrown
Straight to its freedom in the thunderous cloud.

II

WINTER SWAN

It is a hollow garden, under the cloud;
Beneath the heel a hollow earth is turned;
Within the mind the live blood shouts aloud;
Under the breast the willing blood is burned,
Shut with the fire passed and the fire returned.
But speak, you proud!
Where lies the leaf-caught world once thought abiding,
Now but a dry disarray and artifice?
Here, to the ripple cut by the cold, drifts this
Bird, the long throat bent back, and the eyes in hiding.

IF WE TAKE ALL GOLD

If we take all gold
And put all gold by,
Lay by the treasure
In the shelved earth's crevice,
Under, under the deepest,
Store sorrow's gold:
That which we thought precious
And guarded even in sleep
Under the miserly pillow,
If it be hid away
Lost under dark heaped ground,
Then shall we have peace,
Sorrow's gold being taken
From out the clean house,
From the rifled coffers put by.

THE DRUM

The drum roars up.
O blood refused,
Here's your answer.
The ear is used.

A miss and a beat
The skin and the stick
Part and meet,
Gather thick.

Now they part,
Now they're meeting.
There's not on the heart
So much beating.

Use up the air
To the last drop,
To the last layer,
Before you stop.

Whatever is toward
It's the drums I'll have,
Dying a coward
Or living brave.

DIVISION

Long days and changing weather
Put the shadow upon the door:
Up from the ground, the duplicate
Tree reflected in shadow;
Out from the whole, the single
Mirrored against the single.
The tree and the hour and the shadow
No longer mingle,
Fly free, that burned together.

Replica, turned to yourself
Upon thinnest color and air—
Woven in changeless leaves
The burden of the seen
Is clasped against the eye,
Though assailed and undone is the green
Upon the wall and the sky:
Time and the tree stand there.

CASSANDRA

To me, one silly task is like another.
I bare the shambling tricks of lust and pride.
This flesh will never give a child its mother,—
Song, like a wing, tears through my breast, my side,
And madness chooses out my voice again,
Again. I am the chosen no hand saves:
The shrieking heaven lifted over men,
Not the dumb earth, wherein they set their graves.

THE CUPOLA

A mirror hangs on the wall of the draughty cupola.
Within the depths of glass mix the oak and the beech leaf,
Once held to the boughs' shape, but now to the shape of
    the wind.

Someone has hung the mirror here for no reason,
In the shuttered room, an eye for the drifted leaves,
For the oak leaf, the beech, a handsbreadth of darkest reflection.

Someone has thought alike of the bough and the wind
And struck their shape to the wall. Each in its season
Spills negligent death throughout the abandoned chamber.

GIRL'S SONG

Winter, that is a fireless room
In a locked house, was our love's home.
The days turn, and you are not here,
O changing with the little year!

Now when the scent of plants half-grown
Is more the season's than their own
And neither sun nor wind can stanch
The gold forsythia's dripping branch,—

Another maiden, still not I,
Looks from some hill upon some sky,
And, since she loves you, and she must,
Puts her young cheek against the dust.

FEUER-NACHT

The leaf-veined fire,
Sworn to trouble the least
The shuttered eye
Turned from its feast,—
Running the night
In long fanned gush,
Must burn in that sight
Less than a rush.

The torch being laid
And the land kindled,
And the deepest shade
Caught fire-brindled;
The thicket and the bare
Rock, rising bright—
The eye in its lair
Quivers for sight.

To touch at the sedge
And then run tame
Is a broken pledge.
The leaf-shaped flame
Shears the bark piled for winter,
The grass in the stall.
Sworn to lick at a little,
It has burned all.

SECOND SONG

I said out of sleeping:
Passion, farewell.
Take from my keeping
Bauble and shell,

Black salt, black provender.
Tender your store
To a new pensioner,
To me no more.

THE MARK

Where should he seek, to go away
That shadow will not point him down?
The spear of dark in the strong day
Beyond the upright body thrown,
Marking no epoch but its own.

Loosed only when, at noon and night,
The body is the shadow's prison.
The pivot swings into the light;
The center left, the shadow risen
To range out into time's long treason.

Stand pinned to sight, while now, unbidden,
The apple loosens, not at call,
Falls to the field, and lies there hidden,—
Another and another fall
And lie there hidden, in spite of all

The diagram of whirling shade,
The visible, that thinks to spin
Forever webs that time has made
Though momently time wears them thin
And all at length are gathered in.

LATE

The cormorant still screams
Over cave and promontory.
Stony wings and bleak glory
Battle in your dreams.
Now sullen and deranged,
Not simply, as a child,
You look upon the earth
And find it harrowed and wild.
Now, only to mock
At the sterile cliff laid bare,
At the cold pure sky unchanged,
You look upon the rock,
You look upon the air.

SIMPLE AUTUMNAL

The measured blood beats out the year's delay.
The tearless eyes and heart, forbidden grief,
Watch the burned, restless, but abiding leaf,
The brighter branches arming the bright day.

The cone, the curving fruit should fall away,
The vine stem crumble, ripe grain know its sheaf.
Bonded to time, fires should have done, be brief,
But, serfs to sleep, they glitter and they stay.

Because not last nor first, grief in its prime
Wakes in the day, and hears of life's intent.
Sorrow would break the seal stamped over time
And set the baskets where the bough is bent.

Full season's come, yet filled trees keep the sky
And never scent the ground where they must lie.

DARK SUMMER

Under the thunder-dark, the cicadas resound.
The storm in the sky mounts, but is not yet heard.
The shaft and the flash wait, but are not yet found.

The apples that hang and swell for the late comer,
The simple spell, the rite not for our word,
The kisses not for our mouths,—light the dark summer.

DIDACTIC PIECE

The eye unacquitted by whatever it holds in allegiance:
The trees' upcurve thought sacred, the flaked air, sacred and alter-
    able,
The hard bud seen under the lid, not the scorned leaf and the apple—
As once in a swept space, so now with speech in a house,
We think to stand spelled forever, chained to the rigid knocking
Of a heart whose time is its own flesh, momently swung and burning—
This, in peace, as well, though we know the air a combatant
And the word of the heart's wearing time, that it will not do without
    grief.

The limit already traced must be returned to and visited,
Touched, spanned, proclaimed, else the heart's time be all:
The small beaten disk, under the bent shell of stars,
Beside rocks in the road, dust, and the nameless herbs,
Beside rocks in the water, marked by the heeled-back current,
Seeing, in all autumns, the felled leaf betray the wind.

If but the sign of the end is given a room
By the pillared harp, sealed to its rest by hands—
(On the bright strings the hands are almost reflected,
The strings a mirror and light). The head bends to listen,
So that the grief is heard; tears begin and are silenced
Because of the mimic despair, under the figure of laughter.
Let the allegiance go; the tree and the hard bud seed themselves.
The end is set, whether it be sought or relinquished.
We wait, we hear, facing the mask without eyes,
Grief without grief, facing the eyeless music.

FOR A MARRIAGE

She gives most dangerous sight
To keep his life awake:
A sword sharp-edged and bright
That darkness must not break,
Not ever for her sake.

With it he sees, deep-hidden,
The sullen other blade
To every eye forbidden,
That half her life has made,
And until now obeyed.

Now he will know his part:
Tougher than bone or wood,
To clasp on that barbed heart
That once shed its own blood
In its own solitude.

TEARS IN SLEEP

All night the cocks crew, under a moon like day,
And I, in the cage of sleep, on a stranger's breast,
Shed tears, like a task not to be put away—
In the false light, false grief in my happy bed,
A labor of tears, set against joy's undoing.
I would not wake at your word, I had tears to say.
I clung to the bars of the dream and they were said,
And pain's derisive hand had given me rest
From the night giving off flames, and the dark renewing.

THE CROSSED APPLE

I've come to give you fruit from out my orchard,
Of wide report.
I have trees there that bear me many apples
Of every sort:

Clear, streakèd; red and russet; green and golden;
Sour and sweet.
This apple's from a tree yet unbeholden,
Where two kinds meet,—

So that this side is red without a dapple,
And this side's hue
Is clear and snowy. It's a lovely apple.
It is for you.

Within are five black pips as big as peas,
As you will find,
Potent to breed you five great apple trees
Of varying kind:

To breed you wood for fire, leaves for shade,
Apples for sauce.
Oh, this is a good apple for a maid,
It is a cross,

Fine on the finer, so the flesh is tight,
And grained like silk.
Sweet Burning gave the red side, and the white
Is Meadow Milk.

Eat it; and you will taste more than the fruit:
The blossom, too,
The sun, the air, the darkness at the root,
The rain, the dew,

The earth we came to, and the time we flee,
The fire and the breast.
I claim the white part, maiden, that's for me.
You take the rest.

SONG FOR A SLIGHT VOICE

If ever I render back your heart
So long to me delight and plunder,
It will be bound with the firm strings
That men have built the viol under.

Your stubborn, piteous heart, that bent
To be the place where music stood,
Upon some shaken instrument
Stained with the dark of resinous blood,

Will find its place, beyond denial,
Will hear the dance, O be most sure,
Laid on the curved wood of the viol
Or on the struck tambour.

SONNET

Dark, underground, is furnished with the bone;
The tool's lost, and the counter in the game.
Eaten as though by water or by flame
The elaborate craft built up from wood and stone.

Words made of breath, these also are undone,
And greedy sight abolished in its claim.
Light fails from ruin and from wall the same;
The loud sound and pure silence fall as one.

Worn flesh at last is history and treasure
Unto itself; its scars it still can keep,
Received from love, from memory's false measure,
From pain, from the long dream drawn back in sleep.

Attest, poor body, with what scars you have,
That you left life, to come down to the grave.

FIEND'S WEATHER

O embittered joy,
You fiend in fair weather,
Foul winds from secret quarters
Howl here together.

They yell without sleet
And freeze without snow;
Through them the broken Pleiades
And the Brothers show,

And Orion's steel,
And the iron of the Plough.
This is your night, my worthy fiend,
You can triumph now.

In this wind to wrench the eye
And curdle the ear,
The church steeple rises purely to the heavens;
The sky is clear.

And even to-morrow
Stones without disguise
In true-colored fields
Will glitter for your eyes.

I SAW ETERNITY

O beautiful Forever!
O grandiose Everlasting!
Now, now, now,
I break you into pieces,
I feed you to the ground.

O brilliant, O languishing
Cycle of weeping light!
The mice and birds will eat you,
And you will spoil their stomachs
As you have spoiled my mind.

Here, mice, rats,
Porcupines and toads,
Moles, shrews, squirrels,
Weasels, turtles, lizards,—
Here's bright Everlasting!
Here's a crumb of Forever!
Here's a crumb of Forever!

COME, BREAK WITH TIME

Come, break with time,
You who were lorded
By a clock's chime
So ill afforded.
If time is allayed
Be not afraid.

I shall break, if I will.
Break, since you must.
Time has its fill,
Sated with dust.
Long the clock's hand
Burned like a brand.

Take the rocks' speed
And earth's heavy measure.
Let buried seed
Drain out time's pleasure,
Take time's decrees.
Come, cruel ease.

OLD COUNTRYSIDE

Beyond the hour we counted rain that fell
On the slant shutter, all has come to proof.
The summer thunder, like a wooden bell,
Rang in the storm above the mansard roof,

And mirrors cast the cloudy day along
The attic floor; wind made the clapboards creak.
You braced against the wall to make it strong,
A shell against your cheek.

Long since, we pulled brown oak-leaves to the ground
In a winter of dry trees; we heard the cock
Shout its unplaceable cry, the axe's sound
Delay a moment after the axe's stroke.

Far back, we saw, in the stillest of the year,
The scrawled vine shudder, and the rose-branch show
Red to the thorns, and, sharp as sight can bear,
The thin hound's body arched against the snow.

SUMMER WISH

That cry's from the first cuckoo of the year.
I wished before it ceased.

We call up the green to hide us
This hardened month, by no means the beginning
Of the natural year, but of the shortened span
Of leaves upon the earth. We call upon
The weed as well as the flower: groundsel, stellaria.
It is the month to make the summer wish;
It is time to ask
The wish from summer as always: *It will be,*
It will be.
        That tool we have used
So that its haft is smooth; it knows the hand.
Again we lift the wish to its expert uses,
Tired of the bird that calls one long note downward,
And the forest in cast-iron. No longer, no longer,
The season of the lying equinox
Wherein false cock-crow sounds!

In March the shadow
Already falls with a look of summer, fuller
Upon the snow, because the sun at last
Is almost centered. Later, the sprung moss
Is the tree's shadow; under the black spruces

53

It lies where lately snow lay, bred green from the cold
Cast down from melting branches.

FIRST VOICE

A wish like a hundred others.
You cannot, as once, yearn forward. The blood now never
Stirs hot to memory, or to the fantasy
Of love, with which, both early and late, one lies
As with a lover
Now do you suddenly envy
Poor praise you told long since to keep its tongue,
Or pride's acquired accent,—pomposity, arrogance,
That trip in their latinity? With these at heart
You could make a wish, crammed with the nobility
Of error. It would be no use. You cannot
Take yourself in.

SECOND VOICE

Count over what these days have: lilies
Returned in little to an earth unready,
To the sun not accountable;
The hillside mazed and leafless, but through the ground
The leaf from the bulb, the unencouraged green
Heaving the metal earth, presage of thousand
Shapes of young leaves—lanceolate, trefoil,
Peach, willow, plum, the lilac like a heart.

Memory long since put by,—to what end the dream
That drags back lived-out life with the wrong words,
The substitute meaning?
Those that you once knew there play out false time,
Elaborate yesterday's words, that they were deaf to,
Being dead ten years.—Call back in anguish
The anger in childhood that defiled the house
In walls and timber with its violence?
Now must you listen again
To your own tears, shed as a child, hold the bruise
With your hand, and weep, fallen against the wall,
And beg, *Don't, don't,* while the pitiful rage goes on
That cannot stem itself?
Or, having come into woman's full estate,
Enter the rich field, walk between the bitter
Bowed grain, being compelled to serve,
To heed unchecked in the heart the reckless fury
That tears fresh day from day, destroys its traces,—
Now bear the blow too young?

SECOND VOICE

In early April
At six o'clock the sun has not set; on the walls
It shines with scant light, pale, dilute, misplaced,
Light there's no use for. At overcast noon
The sun comes out in a flash, and is taken
Slowly back to the cloud.

FIRST VOICE

Not memory, and not the renewed conjecture
Of passion that opens the breast, the unguarded look
Flaying clean the raped defense of the body,
Breast, bowels, throat, now pulled to the use of the eyes
That see and are taken. The body that works and sleeps,
Made vulnerable, night and day, to delight that changes
Upon the lips that taste it, to the lash of jealousy
Struck on the face, so the betraying bed
Is gashed clear, cold on the mind, together with
Every embrace that agony dreads but sees
Open as the love of dogs.

SECOND VOICE

The cloud shadow flies up the bank, but does not
Blow off like smoke. It stops at the bank's edge.
In the field by trees two shadows come together.
The trees and the cloud throw down their shadow upon
The man who walks there. Dark flows up from his feet
To his shoulders and throat, then has his face in its mask,
Then lifts.

FIRST VOICE

Will you turn to yourself, proud breast,
Sink to yourself, to an ingrained, pitiless
Rejection of voice and touch not your own, press sight
Into a myth no eye can take the gist of;

Clot up the bone of phrase with the black conflict
That claws it back from sense?

                              Go into the breast . . .

You have traced that lie, before this, out to its end,
Heard bright wit headstrong in the beautiful voice
Changed to a word mumbled across the shoulder
To one not there; the gentle self split up
Into a yelling fiend and a soft child.
You have seen the ingrown look
Come at last upon a vision too strong
Ever to turn away.

The breast's six madnesses repeat their dumb-show.

SECOND VOICE

In the bright twilight children call out in the fields.
The evening takes their cry. How late it is!
Around old weeds worn thin and bleached to their pith
The field has leaped to stalk and strawberry blossom.
The orchard by the road
Has the pear-tree full at once of flowers and leaves,
The cherry with flowers only.

FIRST VOICE

The mind for refuge, the grain of reason, the will,
Pulled by a wind it thinks to point and name?

Malicious symbol, key for rusty wards,
The crafty knight in the game, with its mixed move,
Prey to an end not evident to craft. . . .

SECOND VOICE

Fields are ploughed inward
From edge to center; furrows squaring off
Make dark lines far out in irregular fields,
On hills that are builded like great clouds that over them
Rise, to depart.
Furrow within furrow, square within a square,
Draw to the center where the team turns last.
Horses in half-ploughed fields
Make earth they walk upon a changing color.

FIRST VOICE

The year's begun; the share's again in the earth.

Speak out the wish like music, that has within it
The horn, the string, the drum pitched deep as grief.
Speak it like laughter, outward. O brave, O generous
Laughter that pours from the well of the body and draws
The bane that cheats the heart: aconite, nightshade,
Hellebore, hyssop, rue,—symbols and poisons
We drink, in fervor, thinking to gain thereby
Some difference, some distinction.
Speak it, as that man said, *as though the earth spoke,*

By the body of rock, shafts of heaved strata, separate,
Together.
      Though it be but for sleep at night,
Speak out the wish.
The vine we pitied is in leaf; the wild
Honeysuckle blows by the granite.

SECOND VOICE

See now
Open above the field, stilled in wing-stiffened flight,
The stretched hawk fly.

III

SONG

It is not now I learn
To turn the heart away
From the rain of a wet May
Good for the grass and leaves.
Years back I paid my tithe
And earned my salt in kind,
And watched the long slow scythe
Move where the grain is lined,
And saw the stubble burn
Under the darker sheaves.
Whatever now must go
It is not the heart that grieves.
It is not the heart—the stock,
The stone,—the deaf, the blind—
That sees the birds in flock
Steer narrowed to the wind.

HENCEFORTH, FROM THE MIND

Henceforth, from the mind,
For your whole joy, must spring
Such joy as you may find
In any earthly thing,
And every time and place
Will take your thought for grace.

Henceforth, from the tongue,
From shallow speech alone,
Comes joy you thought, when young,
Would wring you to the bone,
Would pierce you to the heart
And spoil its stop and start.

Henceforward, from the shell,
Wherein you heard, and wondered
At oceans like a bell
So far from ocean sundered—
A smothered sound that sleeps
Long lost within lost deeps,

Will chime you change and hours,
The shadow of increase,
Will sound you flowers
Born under troubled peace—
Henceforth, henceforth
Will echo sea and earth.

HOMUNCULUS

O see what I have made!
A delicate precious ruse
By which death is betrayed
And all time given use.

See this fine body, joined
More cleanly than a thorn.
What man, though lusty-loined,
What woman from woman born,

Shaped a slight thing, so strong,
Or a wise thing, so young?
This mouth will yet know song
And words move on this tongue.

It lacks but life: some scent,
Some kernel of hot endeavor,
Some dust of dead content
Will make it live forever.

SINGLE SONNET

Now, you great stanza, you heroic mould,
Bend to my will, for I must give you love:
The weight in the heart that breathes, but cannot move,
Which to endure flesh only makes so bold.

Take up, take up, as it were lead or gold
The burden; test the dreadful mass thereof.
No stone, slate, metal under or above
Earth, is so ponderous, so dull, so cold.

Too long as ocean bed bears up the ocean,
As earth's core bears the earth, have I borne this;
Too long have lovers, bending for their kiss,
Felt bitter force cohering without motion.

Staunch meter, great song, it is yours, at length,
To prove how stronger you are than my strength.

EXHORTATION

Give over seeking bastard joy
Nor cast for fortune's side-long look.
Indifference can be your toy;
The bitter heart can be your book.
(Its lesson torment never shook.)

In the cold heart, as on a page,
Spell out the gentle syllable
That puts short limit to your rage
And curdles the straight fire of hell,
Compassing all, so all is well.

Read how, though passion sets in storm
And grief's a comfort, and the young
Touch at the flint when it is warm,
It is the dead we live among,
The dead given motion, and a tongue.

The dead, long trained to cruel sport
And the crude gossip of the grave;
The dead, who pass in motley sort,
Whom sun nor sufferance can save.
Face them. They sneer. Do not be brave.

Know once for all: their snare is set
Even now; be sure their trap is laid;
And you will see your lifetime yet
Come to their terms, your plans unmade,—
And be belied, and be betrayed.

HYPOCRITE SWIFT

Hypocrite Swift now takes an eldest daughter.
He lifts Vanessa's hand. Cudsho, my dove!
Drink Wexford ale and quaff down Wexford water
But never love.

He buys new caps; he and Lord Stanley ban
Hedge-fellows who have neither wit nor swords.
He turns his coat; Tories are in; Queen Anne
Makes twelve new lords.

The town mows hay in hell; he swims in the river;
His giddiness returns; his head is hot.
Berries are clean, while peaches damn the giver
(Though grapes do not).

Mrs. Vanhomrigh keeps him safe from the weather.
Preferment pulls his periwig askew.
Pox takes belittlers; do the willows feather?
God keep you.

Stella spells ill; Lords Peterborough and Fountain
Talk politics; the Florence wine went sour.
Midnight: two different clocks, here and in Dublin,
Give out the hour.

On walls at court, long gilded mirrors gaze.
The parquet shines; outside the snow falls deep.

Venus, the Muses stare above the maze.
Now sleep.

Dream the mixed, fearsome dream. The satiric word
Dies in its horror. Wake, and live by stealth.
The bitter quatrain forms, is here, is heard,
Is wealth.

What care I; what cares saucy Presto? Stir
The bed-clothes; hearten up the perishing fire.
Hypocrite Swift sent Stella a green apron
And dead desire.

AT A PARTY

Over our heads, if we but knew,
Over our senses, as they reel,
The planets tread, great seven, great two
Venus, Uranus, in a wheel.

Spirit (and let the flesh speak out),
Be still. To make this moment mine
All matter falls into a rout;
Both art and usury combine.

And each bright symbol of their power
Speaks of my triumph, and your fall.
Step forth, then, malice, wisdom's guide,
And enmity, that may save us all.

TO WINE

Cup, ignorant and cruel,
Take from the mandate, love,
Its urgency to prove
Unfaith, renewal.

Take from the mind its loss:
The lipless dead that lie
Face upward in the earth,
Strong hand and slender thigh;
Return to the vein
All that is worth
Grief. Give that beat again.

POEM IN PROSE

I turned from side to side, from image to image, to put you down,
All to no purpose; for you the rhymes would not ring—
Not for you, beautiful and ridiculous, as are always the true inheritors
    of love,
The bearers; their strong hair moulded to their foreheads as though by
    the pressure of hands.
It is you that must sound in me secretly for the little time before my
    mind, schooled in desperate esteem, forgets you—
And it is my virtue that I cannot give you out,
That you are absorbed into my strength, my mettle,
That in me you are matched, and that it is silence which comes from us.

SHORT SUMMARY

Listen but once to the words written out by my hand
In the long line fit only for giving ease
To the tiresome heart. I say: Not again shall we stand
Under green trees.

How we stood, in the early season, but at the end of day,
In the yes of new light, but at the twice-lit hour,
Seeing at one time the shade deepened all one way
And the breaking flower;

Hearing at one time the sound of the night-fall's reach
And that checked breath bound to the mouth and caught
Back to the mouth, closing its mocking speech:
Remind me not.

Soon to dark's mid-most pitch the divided light
Ran. The balance fell, and we were not there.
It was early season; it was the verge of night;
It was our land;
It was evening air.

ITALIAN MORNING

Half circle's come before we know.
Full in the falling arc, we hear
Our heel give earth a lonely blow.
We place the hour and name the year.

High in a room long since designed
For our late visit under night,
We sleep: we wake to watch the lined
Wave take strange walls with counterfeit light.

The big magnolia, like a hand,
Repeats our flesh. (O bred to love,
Gathered to silence!) In a land
Thus garnished, there is time enough

To pace the rooms where painted swags
Of fruit and flower in pride depend,
Stayed as we are not. The hour wags
Deliberate, and great arches bend

In long perspective past our eye.

Mutable body, and brief name,
Confront, against an early sky,
This marble herb, and this stone flame.

MAN ALONE

It is yourself you seek
In a long rage,
Scanning through light and darkness
Mirrors, the page,

Where should reflected be
Those eyes and that thick hair,
That passionate look, that laughter.
You should appear

Within the book, or doubled,
Freed, in the silvered glass;
Into all other bodies
Yourself should pass.

The glass does not dissolve;
Like walls the mirrors stand;
The printed page gives back
Words by another hand.

And your infatuate eye
Meets not itself below:
Strangers lie in your arms
As I lie now.

BAROQUE COMMENT

From loud sound and still chance;
From mindless earth, wet with a dead million leaves;
From the forest, the empty desert, the tearing beasts,
The kelp-disordered beaches;
Coincident with the lie, anger, lust, oppression and death in many
    forms:

Ornamental structures, continents apart, separated by seas;
Fitted marble, swung bells; fruit in garlands as well as on the branch;
The flower at last in bronze, stretched backward, or curled within;
Stone in various shapes: beyond the pyramid, the contrived arch and
    the buttress;
The named constellations;
Crown and vesture; palm and laurel chosen as noble and enduring;
Speech proud in sound; death considered sacrifice;
Mask, weapon, urn; the ordered strings;
Fountains; foreheads under weather-bleached hair;
The wreath, the oar, the tool,
The prow;
The turned eyes and the opened mouth of love.

TO MY BROTHER
KILLED: HAUMONT WOOD:
OCTOBER, 1918

O you so long dead,
You masked and obscure,
I can tell you, all things endure:
The wine and the bread;

The marble quarried for the arch;
The iron become steel;
The spoke broken from the wheel;
The sweat of the long march;

The hay-stacks cut through like loaves
And the hundred flowers from the seed;
All things indeed
Though struck by the hooves

Of disaster, of time due,
Of fell loss and gain,
All things remain,
I can tell you, this is true.

Though burned down to stone
Though lost from the eye,
I can tell you, and not lie,—
Save of peace alone.

THE SLEEPING FURY

You are here now,
Who were so loud and feared, in a symbol before me,
Alone and asleep, and I at last look long upon you.

Your hair fallen on your cheek, no longer in the semblance of serpents,
Lifted in the gale; your mouth, that shrieked so, silent.
You, my scourge, my sister, lie asleep, like a child,
Who, after rage, for an hour quiet, sleeps out its tears.

The days close to winter
Rough with strong sound. We hear the sea and the forest,
And the flames of your torches fly, lit by others,
Ripped by the wind, in the night. The black sheep for sacrifice
Huddle together. The milk is cold in the jars.

All to no purpose, as before, the knife whetted and plunged,
The shout raised, to match the clamor you have given them.
You alone turn away, not appeased; unaltered, avenger.

Hands full of scourges, wreathed with your flames and adders,
You alone turned away, but did not move from my side,
Under the broken light, when the soft nights took the torches.

At thin morning you showed, thick and wrong in that calm,
The ignoble dream and the mask, sly, with slits at the eyes,
Pretence and half-sorrow, beneath which a coward's hope trembled.

You uncovered at night, in the locked stillness of houses,
False love due the child's heart, the kissed-out lie, the embraces,
Made by the two who for peace tenderly turned to each other.

You who know what we love, but drive us to know it;
You with your whips and shrieks, bearer of truth and of solitude;
You who give, unlike men, to expiation your mercy.

Dropping the scourge when at last the scourged advances to meet it,
You, when the hunted turns, no longer remain the hunter
But stand silent and wait, at last returning his gaze.

Beautiful now as a child whose hair, wet with rage and tears
Clings to its face. And now I may look upon you,
Having once met your eyes. You lie in sleep and forget me.
Alone and strong in my peace, I look upon you in yours.

ROMAN FOUNTAIN

Up from the bronze, I saw
Water without a flaw
Rush to its rest in air,
Reach to its rest, and fall.

Bronze of the blackest shade,
An element man-made,
Shaping upright the bare
Clear gouts of water in air.

O, as with arm and hammer,
Still it is good to strive
To beat out the image whole,
To echo the shout and stammer
When full-gushed waters, alive,
Strike on the fountain's bowl
After the air of summer.

RHYME

What laid, I said,
My being waste?
'Twas your sweet flesh
With its sweet taste,—

Which, like a rose,
Fed with a breath,
And at its full
Belied all death.

It's at springs we drink;
It's bread we eat,
And no fine body,
Head to feet,

Should force all bread
And drink together,
Nor be both sun
And hidden weather.

Ah no, it should not;
Let it be.
But once heart's feast
You were to me.

M., SINGING

Now, innocent, within the deep
Night of all things you turn the key,
Unloosing what we know in sleep.
In your fresh voice they cry aloud
Those beings without heart or name.

Those creatures both corrupt and proud,
Upon the melancholy words
And in the music's subtlety,
Leave the long harvest which they reap
In the sunk land of dust and flame
And move to space beneath our sky.

EVENING-STAR

Light from the planet Venus, soon to set,
Be with us.

Light, pure and round, without heat or shadow,
Held in the cirrus sky, at evening:
Accompany what we do.

Be with us;
Know our partial strength.
Serve us in your own way,
Brief planet, shining without burning.

Light, lacking words that might praise you;
Wanting and breeding sighs only.

PUTTING TO SEA

Who, in the dark, has cast the harbor-chain?
This is no journey to a land we know.
The autumn night receives us, hoarse with rain;
Storm flakes with roaring foam the way we go.

Sodden with summer, stupid with its loves,
The country which we leave, and now this bare
Circle of ocean which the heaven proves
Deep as its height, and barren with despair.

Now this whole silence, through which nothing breaks,
Now this whole sea, which we possess alone,
Flung out from shore with speed a missile takes
When some hard hand, in hatred, flings a stone.

The Way should mark our course within the night,
The streaming System, turned without a sound.
What choice is this—profundity and flight—
Great sea? Our lives through we have trod the ground.

Motion beneath us, fixity above.

"O, but you should rejoice! The course we steer
Points to a beach bright to the rocks with love,
Where, in hot calms, blades clatter on the ear;

And spiny fruits up through the earth are fed
With fire; the palm trees clatter; the wave leaps.

Fleeing a shore where heart-loathed love lies dead
We point lands where love fountains from its deeps.

Through every season the coarse fruits are set
In earth not fed by streams." Soft into time
Once broke the flower: pear and violet,
The cinquefoil. The tall elm tree and the lime

Once held out fruitless boughs, and fluid green
Once rained about us, pulse of earth indeed.
There, out of metal, and to light obscene,
The flamy blooms burn backwards to their seed.

With so much hated still so close behind
The sterile shores before us must be faced;
Again, against the body and the mind,
The hate that bruises, though the heart is braced.

Bend to the chart, in the extinguished night
Mariners! Make way slowly; stay from sleep;
That we may have short respite from such light.

And learn, with joy, the gulf, the vast, the deep.

SPIRIT'S SONG

How well you served me above ground,
Most truthful sight, firm-builded sound.

And how you throve through hunger, waste,
Sickness and health, informing taste;

And smell, that did from dung and heather,
Corruption, bloom, mix well together.

But you, fierce delicate tender touch,
Betrayed and hurt me overmuch,

For whom I lagged with what a crew
O far too long, and poisoned through!

KEPT

Time for the wood, the clay,
The trumpery dolls, the toys
Now to be put away:
We are not girls and boys.

What are these rags we twist
Our hearts upon, or clutch
Hard in the sweating fist?
They are not worth so much.

But we must keep such things
Till we at length begin
To feel our nerves their strings,
Their dust, our blood within.

The dreadful painted bisque
Becomes our very cheek.
A doll's heart, faint at risk,
Within our breast grows weak.

Our hand the doll's, our tongue.

Time for the pretty clay,
Time for the straw, the wood.
The playthings of the young
Get broken in the play,
Get broken, as they should.

HEARD BY A GIRL

Something said: You have nothing to fear
From those long fine bones, and that beautiful ear.

From the mouth, and the eyes set well apart,
There's nothing can come which will break your heart.

From the simple voice, the indulgent mind,
No venom breeds to defeat your kind.

And even, it said, those hands are thin
And large, well designed to clasp within

Their fingers (and O what more do you ask?)
The secret and the delicate mask.

PACKET OF LETTERS

In the shut drawer, even now, they rave and grieve—
To be approached at times with the frightened tear;
Their cold to be drawn away from, as one, at nightfall,
Draws the cloak closer against the cold of the marsh.

There, there, the thugs of the heart did murder.
There, still in murderers' guise, two stand embraced, embalmed.

SONG FOR A LYRE

The landscape where I lie
Again from boughs sets free
Summer; all night must fly
In wind's obscurity
The thick, green leaves that made
Heavy the August shade.

Soon, in the pictured night,
Returns—as in a dream
Left after sleep's delight—
The shallow autumn stream:
Softly awake, its sound
Poured on the chilly ground.

Soon fly the leaves in throngs;
O love, though once I lay
Far from its sound, to weep,
When night divides my sleep,
When stars, the autumn stream,
Stillness, divide my dream,
Night to your voice belongs.

IV

SEVERAL VOICES OUT OF A CLOUD

Come, drunks and drug-takers; come, perverts unnerved!
Receive the laurel, given, though late, on merit; to whom
    and wherever deserved.

Parochial punks, trimmers, nice people, joiners true-blue,
Get the hell out of the way of the laurel. It is deathless
    And it isn't for you.

ANIMAL, VEGETABLE AND MINERAL

Glass Flowers from the Ware Collection in the Botanical
Museum of Harvard University. Insect Pollination Series,
with Sixteen Color Plates, by Fritz Kredel. New York:
Harcourt, Brace and Company. 58 pages. $1.50.

    Dieu ne croit pas à notre Dieu. JULES RENARD

On gypsum slabs of preternatural whiteness
In Cambridge (Mass.) on Oxford Street is laid
One craft wherein great Nature needs no aid
From man's Abstracts and Concretes, Wrong and
   Rightness:
Cross-pollination's fixed there and displayed.

Interdependence of the seed and hive!
Astounding extraverted bee and flower!
Mixture of styles! Intensity of drive!
Both Gothic and Baroque blooms flaunt their power.
The classic *Empire* bees within them strive.

The flower is to bee a kind of arrow;
Nectar is pointed out by spot and line.
Corollas may be shaped both wide and narrow;
Mechanics vary, though the play is fine,
And bee-adapted (not for crow or sparrow).

Bush-bean and butterwort keep bee in mind;
Chamisso too (which has no common name);
Red larkspur, devil's-bit scabious are aligned
With garden violet in this bee-ish claim
(*Impatiens Roylei Walpers* acts the same).

Expectancy is constant; means are shifting.
One flower has black cloven glands that pinch
The bee's foot (on the stigma these are lifting);
Anthers with cell-hid pollen wait the clinch.
Think well on this, who think that Life is Drifting . . .

Eager quickly to free its sticky foot
The bee stamps briskly just where stamp is needed:
Motion and power attendant on this boot
Extract *pollinia*. (Here the mind's exceeded;
Wild intimations through the fibers shoot.)

Self-fertile flowers are feeble and need priming.
Nature is for this priming, it appears.
Some flowers, like water-clocks, have perfect timing:
Pistil and anthers rise, as though on gears;
One's up and when t'other's down; one falls; one's
    climbing.

Charles Darwin saw the primrose, and took thought.
Later, he watched the orchids. There, the bees
Enter in, one way; then, with pollen fraught,
Have to climb out another, on their knees.
The stigma profits, and the plant's at ease.

The dyer's greenwood waits the bee in tension.
Petals are pressed down: then the stamens spring
(The pistils, too) into a new dimension,

Hitting the bee's back between wing and wing.
Who thought this out? It passes comprehension.

For forty million years this has gone on
(So Baltic amber shows, and can it lie?)
The bee's back, feet, head, belly have been drawn
Into the flower's plan for history.
Nectar's been yielded for the hexagon.

Then think of Blaschkas (*père et fils*), who spent
Full fifty years in delicate adjusting,
Glass-blowing, molding, skill with instrument,
While many other crafts were merely rusting.
Two Yankee Wares (*mère, fille*) the money lent.

Cynics who think all this *bijouterie*
Certainly lack a Deepening Sense of Awe.
Here Darwin, Flora, Blaschkas and the bee
Fight something out that ends in a close draw
Above the cases howls loud mystery.

What is the chain, then ask, and what the links?
Are these acts sad or droll? From what derived?
Within the floret's disk the insect drinks.
Next summer there's more honey to be hived.

What Artist laughs? What clever Daemon thinks?

QUESTION IN A FIELD

Pasture, stone wall, and steeple,
What most perturbs the mind:
The heart-rending homely people,
Or the horrible beautiful kind?

SOLITARY OBSERVATION BROUGHT BACK FROM A SOJOURN IN HELL

At midnight tears
Run into your ears.

VARIATION ON A SENTENCE

There are few or no bluish animals . . .
Thoreau's Journals, Feb. 21, 1855

Of white and tawny, black as ink,
Yellow, and undefined, and pink,
And piebald, there are droves, I think.

(Buff kine in herd, gray whales in pod,
Brown woodchucks, colored like the sod,
All creatures from the hand of God.)

And many of a hellish hue;
But, for some reason hard to view,
Earth's bluish animals are few.

V

THE DREAM

O God, in the dream the terrible horse began
To paw at the air, and make for me with his blows.
Fear kept for thirty-five years poured through his mane,
And retribution equally old, or nearly, breathed through
    his nose.

Coward complete, I lay and wept on the ground
When some strong creature appeared, and leapt for the
    rein.
Another woman, as I lay half in a swound,
Leapt in the air, and clutched at the leather and chain.

Give him, she said, something of yours as a charm.
Throw him, she said, some poor thing you alone claim.
No, no, I cried, he hates me; he's out for harm,
And whether I yield or not, it is all the same.

But, like a lion in a legend, when I flung the glove
Pulled from my sweating, my cold right hand,
The terrible beast, that no one may understand,
Came to my side, and put down his head in love.

TO AN ARTIST, TO TAKE HEART

Slipping in blood, by his own hand, through pride,
Hamlet, Othello, Coriolanus fall.
Upon his bed, however, Shakespeare died,
Having endured them all.

TO BE SUNG ON THE WATER

Beautiful, my delight,
Pass, as we pass the wave.
Pass, as the mottled night
Leaves what it cannot save,
Scattering dark and bright.

Beautiful, pass and be
Less than the guiltless shade
To which our vows were said;
Less than the sound of the oar
To which our vows were made,—
Less than the sound of its blade
Dipping the stream once more.

MUSICIAN

Where have these hands been,
By what delayed,
That so long stayed
Apart from the thin

Strings which they now grace
With their lonely skill?
Music and their cool will
At last interlace.

Now with great ease, and slow,
The thumb, the finger, the strong
Delicate hand plucks the long
String it was born to know.

And, under the palm, the string
Sings as it wished to sing.

CARTOGRAPHY

As you lay in sleep
I saw the chart
Of artery and vein
Running from your heart,

Plain as the strength
Marked upon the leaf
Along the length,
Mortal and brief,

Of your gaunt hand.
I saw it clear:
The wiry brand
Of the life we bear

Mapped like the great
Rivers that rise
Beyond our fate
And distant from our eyes.

"COME, SLEEP . . ."

The bee's fixed hexagon;
The ant's downward tower;
The whale's effortless eating;
The palm's love; the flower

Burnished like brass, clean like wax
Under the pollen;
The rough grass-blade upright;
The smooth swathe fallen:

Do the shadows of these forms and appetites
Repeat, when these lives give over,
In sleep, the rôle of the selfish devourer,
The selfless lover?

Surely, whispers in the glassy corridor
Never trouble their dream.
Never, for them, the dark turreted house reflects itself
In the depthless stream.

ZONE

We have struck the regions wherein we are keel or reef.
The wind breaks over us,
And against high sharp angles almost splits into words,
And these are of fear or grief.

Like a ship, we have struck expected latitudes
Of the universe, in March.
Through one short segment's arch
Of the zodiac's round
We pass,
Thinking: Now we hear
What we heard last year,
And bear the wind's rude touch
And its ugly sound
Equally with so much
We have learned how to bear.

KAPUZINERBERG (SALZBURG)

(from the French of Pierre-Jean Jouve)

From the low eighteenth-century window—its thicknesses of pane and blind shut against the sun, its silence, the odor of summer through it—from the low window which reminds one so deliciously of Goethe retired, working, inspiring all Germany—from there—the cascades of hot trees in a morning already sick with future heat.

The great elms and chestnut trees of the garden falling one below the other do not blot out the view. To the right, the plain opening on Bavaria; opposite, a mixture of extraordinary mountains and convents and bell-towers; to the left the squat Schloss which rises from another part of the town and from this point seems to adhere to the pale sky, through branches which are green banks of the atmosphere.

The town is invisible. But from this small airy house where I stand, it is so good to remember it! Beautiful faces of the centuries, how charming you are. Thoughts of all piteous men, and of those worthy of attention, beyond time and frontiers, how I love you.

EVENING IN THE SANITARIUM*

The free evening fades, outside the windows fastened with decorative
    iron grilles.
The lamps are lighted; the shades drawn; the nurses are watching a
    little.
It is the hour of the complicated knitting on the safe bone needles; of
    the games of anagrams and bridge;
The deadly game of chess; the book held up like a mask.

The period of the wildest weeping, the fiercest delusion, is over.
The women rest their tired half-healed hearts; they are almost well.
Some of them will stay almost well always: the blunt-faced woman
    whose thinking dissolved
Under academic discipline; the manic-depressive girl
Now leveling off; one paranoiac afflicted with jealousy.
Another with persecution. Some alleviation has been possible.

O fortunate bride, who never again will become elated after childbirth!
O lucky older wife, who has been cured of feeling unwanted!
To the suburban railway station you will return, return,
To meet forever Jim home on the 5:35.
You will be again as normal and selfish and heartless as anybody else.

There is life left: the piano says it with its octave smile.
The soft carpets pad the thump and splinter of the suicide to be.
Everything will be splendid: the grandmother will not drink habitually.
The fruit salad will bloom on the plate like a bouquet
And the garden produce the blue-ribbon aquilegia.

* This poem was originally published with the subtitle "Imitated from Auden."

The cats will be glad; the fathers feel justified; the mothers relieved.
The sons and husbands will no longer need to pay the bills.
Childhoods will be put away, the obscene nightmare abated.

At the ends of the corridors the baths are running.
Mrs. C. again feels the shadow of the obsessive idea.
Miss R. looks at the mantel-piece, which must mean something.

FROM HEINE

Der Tod, das ist die kühle Nacht . . .

Death is the tranquil night.
Life is the sultry day.
It darkens; I will sleep now;
The light has made me weary.

Over my bed rises a tree
Wherein sings the young nightingale.
It sings of constant love.
Even in this dream I hear it.

THE DAEMON

Must I tell again
In the words I know
For the ears of men
The flesh, the blow?

Must I show outright
The bruise in the side,
The halt in the night,
And how death cried?

Must I speak to the lot
Who little bore?
It said *Why not?*
It said *Once more.*

AFTER THE PERSIAN

I

I do not wish to know
The depths of your terrible jungle:
From what nest your leopard leaps
Or what sterile lianas are at once your serpents' disguise
        and home.

I am the dweller on the temperate threshold,
The strip of corn and vine,
Where all is translucence (the light!)
Liquidity, and the sound of water.
Here the days pass under shade
And the nights have the waxing and the waning moon.
Here the moths take flight at evening;
Here at morning the dove whistles and the pigeons coo.
Here, as night comes on, the fireflies wink and snap
Close to the cool ground,
Shining in a profusion
Celestial or marine.

Here it is never wholly dark but always wholly green,
And the day stains with what seems to be more than the
        sun
What may be more than my flesh.

II

I have wept with the spring storm;
Burned with the brutal summer.
Now, hearing the wind and the twanging bow-strings,
I know what winter brings.

The hunt sweeps out upon the plain
And the garden darkens.
They will bring the trophies home
To bleed and perish
Beside the trellis and the lattices,
Beside the fountain, still flinging diamond water,
Beside the pool
(Which is eight-sided, like my heart).

III

All has been translated into treasure:
Weightless as amber,
Translucent as the currant on the branch,
Dark as the rose's thorn.

Where is the shimmer of evil?
This is the shell's iridescence
And the wild bird's wing.

IV

Ignorant, I took up my burden in the wilderness.
Wise with great wisdom, I shall lay it down upon flowers.

V

Goodbye, goodbye!
There was so much to love, I could not love it all;
I could not love it enough.

Some things I overlooked, and some I could not find.
Let the crystal clasp them
When you drink your wine, in autumn.

TRAIN TUNE

Back through clouds
Back through clearing
Back through distance
Back through silence

Back through groves
Back through garlands
Back by rivers
Back below mountains

Back through lightning
Back through cities
Back through stars
Back through hours

Back through plains
Back through flowers
Back through birds
Back through rain

Back through smoke
Back through noon
Back along love
Back through midnight

SONG FOR THE LAST ACT

Now that I have your face by heart, I look.
Less at its features than its darkening frame
Where quince and melon, yellow as young flame,
Lie with quilled dahlias and the shepherd's crook.
Beyond, a garden. There, in insolent ease
The lead and marble figures watch the show
Of yet another summer loath to go
Although the scythes hang in the apple trees.

Now that I have your voice by heart, I look.

Now that I have your voice by heart, I read
In the black chords upon a dulling page
Music that is not meant for music's cage,
Whose emblems mix with words that shake and bleed.
The staves are shuttled over with a stark
Unprinted silence. In a double dream
I must spell out the storm, the running stream.
The beat's too swift. The notes shift in the dark.

Now that I have your voice by heart, I read.

Now that I have your heart by heart, I see
The wharves with their great ships and architraves;
The rigging and the cargo and the slaves
On a strange beach under a broken sky.
O not departure, but a voyage done!
The bales stand on the stone; the anchor weeps

Its red rust downward, and the long vine creeps
Beside the salt herb, in the lengthening sun.

Now that I have your heart by heart, I see.

VI

THE DRAGONFLY

You are made of almost nothing
But of enough
To be great eyes
And diaphanous double vans;
To be ceaseless movement,
Unending hunger
Grappling love.

Link between water and air,
Earth repels you.
Light touches you only to shift into iridescence
Upon your body and wings.

Twice-born, predator,
You split into the heat.
Swift beyond calculation or capture
You dart into the shadow
Which consumes you.

You rocket into the day.
But at last, when the wind flattens the grasses,
For you, the design and purpose stop.

And you fall
With the other husks of summer.

ST. CHRISTOPHER*

A raw-boned and an ignorant man
Keeps ferry, but a man of nerve.
His freight a Child and a Child's toy
(Which is our globe, you will observe.)

But what a look of intent love!
This is the look we do not see
In manners or in mimicry.
Strength's a derivative thereof.

The middle class is what we are.
Poised as a brigand or a barber
The tough young saint, Saint Christopher,
Brings the Child in to the safe harbor.

* Fresco, 15th century copy, variously attributed, after the large St. Christopher, now destroyed, formerly on the façade of San Miniato fra le Torri, attributed by Vasari and others to Antonio Pollaiuolo; Metropolitan Museum.

THE SORCERER'S DAUGHTER

In that situation, all the signs were right: scars
On corresponding thumbs, our two heights in proportion
To an inch. And old remembered songs kept hitting the ear
Portentously, as never before or since.

The meeting was timed to the minute, and was almost missed,
Which gave it the full fillip of being destiny's own.
It was in the stars, on the cards, in the hand;
It couldn't have been otherwise.

The train pulled out of the station, and we were in it.
The boat pulled away from the wharf, and we were on board.

But this series of events had no good auguries about it: no birds flew
        into fortunate quarters
When the knock came upon the door. Matter did not creak or space
        mutter.
Nothing fell up or down; the weather did not give it much help,
And time and place were always wrong.

It was crossed from the start
With all the marks of luck changing
From better to worse.
And by these tokens I begin to think it is mine.

THE YOUNG MAGE

The young mage said:
Make free, make free,
With the wild eagles planing in the mountains
And the serpent in the sea.

The young mage said:
Delight, delight,
In the vine's triumph over marble
And the wind at night.

And he said: Hold
Fast to the leaves' silver
And the flowers' gold.

And he said: Beware
Of the round web swinging from the angle
Of the steep stair,
And of the comet's hair.

MARCH TWILIGHT

This light is loss backward; delight by hurt and by bias gained;
Nothing we know about and all that we shan't have.
It is the light which presages to the loser luck,
And cowardice to the brave.

The hour when the oldest and the newest thoughts begin;
Light shed for the most desperate and kindest embrace.
A watcher in these new, late beams might well see another face
And look into Time's eye, as into a strange house, for what lies within.

JULY DAWN

It was a waning crescent
Dark on the wrong side
On which one does not wish
Setting in the hour before daylight
For my sleepless eyes to look at.

O, as a symbol of dis-hope
Over the July fields,
Dissolving, waning.
In spite of its sickle shape.

I saw it and thought it new
In that short moment
That makes all symbols lucky
Before we read them rightly.

Down to the dark it swam,
Down to the dark it moved,
Swift to that cluster of evenings
When curved toward the full it sharpens.

THE MEETING

For years I thought I knew, at the bottom of the dream,
Who spoke but to say farewell,
Whose smile dissolved, after his first words
Gentle and plausible.

Each time I found him, it was always the same:
Recognition and surprise,
And then the silence, after the first words,
And the shifting of the eyes.

Then the moment when he had nothing to say
And only smiled again,
But this time toward a place beyond me, where I could not stay—
No world of men.

Now I am not sure. Who are you? Who have you been?
Why do our paths cross?
At the deepest bottom of the dream you are let in,
A symbol of loss.

Eye to eye we look, and we greet each other
Like friends from the same land.
Bitter compliance! Like a faithless brother
You take and drop my hand.

NIGHT

The cold remote islands
And the blue estuaries
Where what breathes, breathes
The restless wind of the inlets,
And what drinks, drinks
The incoming tide;

Where shell and weed
Wait upon the salt wash of the sea,
And the clear nights of stars
Swing their lights westward
To set behind the land;

Where the pulse clinging to the rocks
Renews itself forever;
Where, again on cloudless nights,
The water reflects
The firmament's partial setting;

—O remember
In your narrowing dark hours
That more things move
Than blood in the heart.

MORNING

1.

The robins' green-blue eggs
Being the complementary color
To the robins' rosy breast—
Is it a vision in the eye, a resolution in the blood
That calls back these birds, to cherish and to guard?

2.

The clever and as though instructed
Tendril of convolvulus
Having chosen the rosebranch for the support of its
                       ascending spiral
Succeeds in avoiding
All but the smaller thorns.

THREE SONGS

LITTLE LOBELIA'S SONG

I was once a part
Of your blood and bone.
Now no longer—
I'm alone, I'm alone.

Each day, at dawn,
I come out of your sleep;
I can't get back.
I weep, I weep.

Not lost but abandoned,
Left behind;
This is my hand
Upon your mind.

I know nothing.
I can barely speak.
But these are my tears
Upon your cheek.

You look at your face
In the looking glass.
This is the face
My likeness has.

Give me back your sleep
Until you die,
Else I weep, weep,
Else I cry, cry.

Those
Concerning whom they have never spoken and thought never to
    speak;
That place
Hidden, preserved,
That even the exquisite eye of the soul
Cannot completely see.
But they are there:
Those people, and that house, and that evening, seen
Newly above the dividing window sash—
The young will broken
And all time to endure.

Those hours when murderous wounds are made,
Often in joy.

I hear.
But far away are the mango trees (*the mangrove swamps, the
    mandrake root . . .*)
And the thickets of—are they palms?
I watch them as though at the edge of sleep.
I often journey toward them in a boat without oars,
Trusting to rudder and sail.
Coming to the shore, I step out of the boat; I leave it to its anchor;
And I walk fearlessly through ripples of both water and sand.
Then the shells and the pebbles are beneath my feet.

Then these, too, recede,
And I am on firm dry land, with, closely waiting,
A hill all sifted over with shade
Wherein the silence waits.

Farewell, phantoms of flesh and of ocean!
Vision of earth
Heal and receive me.

MASKED WOMAN'S SONG

Before I saw the tall man
Few women should see,
Beautiful and imposing
Was marble to me.

And virtue had its place
And evil its alarms,
But not for that worn face,
And not in those roped arms.

DUE